SOCIAL STUDIES ASSESSMENT

GRADES 5-6

Written by

Concetta Doti Ryan, M.A.

Editor:
Ina Massler Levin, M.A.

Senior Editor:
Sharon Coan, M.S. Ed.

Art Direction:
Elayne Roberts
Darlene Spivak

Illustrator:
Sue Fullam

Product Manager:
Phil Garcia

Imaging:
Alfred Lau
Graphics Plus

Cover Photo:
Image provided by
PhotoDisc ©1994

Publishers:
Rachelle Cracchiolo, M.S. Ed.
Mary Dupuy Smith, M.S. Ed.

Teacher Created Materials, Inc.
P.O. Box 1040
Huntington Beach, CA 92647
©1994 Teacher Created Materials, Inc.
Made in U.S. A.
ISBN 1-55734-780-8

Teacher Created Materials

Table of Contents

Introduction

Recently there have been many changes in the way we teach social studies. The focus is no longer on reading the textbook from front cover to back and taking multiple choice tests. Instead we are making dramatic efforts to get students more interested and involved in the study of social studies. How are we doing this? We are supplementing the textbook with historical fiction, research projects, and cooperative investigations to name a few.

As our focus changes from memorizing facts to deepening our understanding of historical events it becomes necessary to reevaluate our tools of assessment. Do standardized tests, really measure what we as teachers, parents, and students need to know? Essentially what these tests really measure is the student's response to isolated, disconnected questions. In order to get a more complete picture of the students' progress, a more authentic form of assessment is needed, one that is in line with the new methods we are using to teach social studies. Fortunately, there are now several types of assessment that really look at a student's social studies concept development in a sophisticated, detailed, authentic manner.

Portfolios, one of the first types of authentic assessment to gain ground, are an asset to many teachers. Teachers like them because they feel they can control the learning process. In other words, there are no specific rules for portfolios. You design the portfolio to match the needs of your students, your classroom, and your assessment procedures.

Recently, other types of authentic assessment are gaining popularity, particularly performance assessment. Performance assessment is a means to evaluate students in a variety of contexts. It allows them to demonstrate their understanding of concepts and apply knowledge and skills they have acquired.

While many teachers acknowledge that diving into authentic assessment is no easy task, it is certainly worth the effort. Fortunately, resource guides such as this one are making it easier for teachers to use more authentic types of assessment in their classrooms

Introduction *(cont.)*

This resource guide will help you to implement authentic assessment in your classroom immediately. It provides both theoretical information and ideas for practical application. The types of authentic assessment covered in this resource guide include:

★ **Portfolios**

★ **Logs and Journals**

★ **Performance Assessment and Rubrics**

★ **Cooperative Investigations**

★ **Research Projects**

★ **Student Self-Evaluation**

★ **Parent Evaluation**

Along with these sections you will find information about Social Studies Program Evaluation and Social Studies Skills and Concepts Development Evaluation. Each section begins with "Getting Started." Here you will find the following topics:

Rationale: Theoretical information on that particular type of authentic assessment.

How to: Ideas for how to implement that particular type of authentic assessment.

Using the Forms in This Section: Instructions for using every assessment form included in that particular section.

For each type of authentic assessment included in this resource guide, you will find many blackline forms for immediate use in your classroom. There is also a generic record sheet, a student award form, and a social studies assessment bibliography included at the end of the book.

With this extensive resource guide, you should feel confident about implementing an authentic assessment program in your classroom. It will prove worthwhile to you, the parents, and most of all, your students!

Getting Started _____

Rationale

As you transition from a more traditional type of assessment to authentic assessment in social studies, it may be necessary for you to carefully examine the types of supplemental materials you use, activities you assign, units of study, your own methods of teaching, and your personal beliefs about assessment.

Have you ever become frustrated by your students' lack of interest in social studies? You are not alone! In 1988, a study reported that students at all grade levels identified social studies as their most boring class and cited texts as one of the major reasons for this. In order to "turn kids on" to social studies, it is necessary to go beyond mere memorization of facts from the textbook. This can be done by supplementing the text with different types of literature and primary sources. Among the types of literature to include in your social studies program are biographies, historical fiction, myths, and legends. Primary sources include items such as letters, speeches, and diaries.

We also need to provide more authentic projects that allow students to take an active role in their study of social studies. Students can be encouraged to do research projects that require them to go into the community and interview residents about a certain issue or topic. Their findings could then be written up in a report or used as part of a larger project involving the results of research from several students. These types of supplements and activities will make social studies come alive for students.

How to Evaluate Your Social Studies Program

There are several items to consider when evaluating your social studies program. Many of these were mentioned above. You should consider the types of literature and primary sources you use to supplement the text, the types of activities and projects you assign and the types of visual supplements you use to help students to understand the skills in using tools such as maps, globes, and time lines.

You may also choose to do a self-evaluation. If we want students to take part in their evaluation, why not become involved in our own? Consider what you are teaching, why you are teaching it, and how you are teaching it. Then, consider how you assess what you teach. Does your assessment tool measure what you need it to measure?

Getting Started (cont.)

Also consider evaluating the thematic units you use. Do they support the curriculum in the textbook? Was the unit successful with the students? By evaluating these units you will be better prepared to plan your curriculum for the next school year.

Using the Forms in This Section

Social Studies Activity Assessment, Page 7

Evaluate the supplements you use and the activities you assign by answering "yes" or "no" to the simple questions included on this activity assessment page.

Teacher Self-Evaluation, Page 8

It is not always easy to look at our own teaching with a critical eye. However, by doing so we can gain insight into the program we provide for our students. This self-evaluation will ask you to consider the choices you give students, expectations for your students, and your communication skills to name just a few.

Personal Beliefs About Assessment, Page 9

Before deciding which types of authentic assessment you want to implement in your classroom, it is important to think about your beliefs and goals about assessment. Use this form to note your own personal beliefs and goals for social studies assessment in your classroom. Several example statements are given below.

Evaluation needs to be: on-going, informal and formal, clearly defined, noncompetitive.

Evaluation procedures should be: based on daily observations, include process and product, consider parent and student input.

Thematic Unit Evaluation, Page 10

This form is designed to assist you in keeping track of your thematic units, their degree of success, and changes you may wish to make for the following year.

Ancient Greece Thematic Unit

Social Studies Activity Assessment

Check "yes" or "no" to each item.

	YES	NO
Use of Literature		
Biographies	_____	_____
Myths	_____	_____
Historical Fiction	_____	_____
Legends	_____	_____
Poems	_____	_____
Use of Original Documents/ Primary Sources		
Newspaper Accounts	_____	_____
Court Decisions	_____	_____
Letters	_____	_____
Speeches	_____	_____
Diaries	_____	_____
Other Official Documents	_____	_____
Interactive Projects/Activities		
Oral History Projects	_____	_____
Debates	_____	_____
Simulations	_____	_____
Role Playing	_____	_____
Cooperative Learning Tasks	_____	_____
Research Projects	_____	_____
Interviews	_____	_____
Journal Writing	_____	_____
Use of Visual Supplements		
Maps	_____	_____
Globe	_____	_____
Time lines	_____	_____
Charts	_____	_____
Diagrams	_____	_____

Teacher Self-Evaluation

Answer "yes" or "no" to each question.

_____ Does social studies have a significant role in my curriculum?

_____ Do I use historical fiction to supplement the text?

_____ Do I use primary sources to supplement the text?

_____ Do I provide assignments that require critical thinking skills?

_____ Do I ask open-ended questions?

_____ Do I listen carefully to students' responses?

_____ Do I respect students' responses?

_____ Do I have high expectations for all students?

_____ Do I thoroughly explain evaluation criteria?

_____ Do students in the class feel successful?

_____ Do I comment on students' strengths?

_____ Do I offer suggestions for improvement?

_____ Do I provide time for student interaction and sharing?

_____ Do I encourage students to take responsibility for their learning?

_____ Do I allow students to self-evaluate?

_____ Do I encourage parents to participate in the evaluation process of their child?

_____ Do I communicate effectively with students?

_____ Do I communicate effectively with parents?

My strengths are: _____

_____

_____

I would like to improve: _____

_____

_____

_____

Personal Beliefs About Assessment

Use this form to note your own personal beliefs and goals for social studies assessment in your classroom. For sample statements, see page 6.

BELIEFS:	**GOALS:**
Evaluation needs to be...	Evaluation procedures should...

Thematic Unit Evaluation

Unit Title	Unit Description	Date	Degree of Success	Changes For Next Year

10

Getting Started_____

Rationale

It is important that we look at the students' understanding of social studies skills and concepts over time. By making sure that we are covering the necessary skills, we can be assured that students are understanding larger social studies concepts. Therefore, we should keep close record of required grade level skills, the unit these skills are covered in, and how we assess these skills. We should then take careful note of student's concept development, at least once each quarter, so that progress and growth can be tracked and encouraged. This need not be a time consuming process. In fact, completing a simple checklist can be as easy as 1-2-3.

How to Evaluate Social Studies Skills and Concepts

Your first step in this process is to identify the necessary skills you are required to teach at your grade level. A comprehensive checklist of skills for both grades 5 and 6 is provided in this resource guide. Grade 5 can be found on pages 13 through 18. Grade 6 can be found on pages 19 through 24.

After you have charted the skills you are teaching, you can begin observing students for evidence of understanding of larger social studies concepts. Students should be "watched" or observed in a variety of settings doing a variety of activities. Observe them during instructional time, free time, working by themselves, with partners, in small groups, and with best friends. Observe students anywhere and anytime you can! As you observe students, make marks on the comprehensive checklist on pages 25 through 27 to indicate what you saw at that particular time.

Getting Started *(cont.)*

Using the Forms in This Section

Social Studies Skills Checklist Grade 5, Page 13

This comprehensive checklist identifies grade level 5 social studies skills for 14 different strands including: history, geography, economics, culture, ethics and belief systems, social and political systems, national identity, constitutional heritage, citizenship, study skills, visual learning, map and globe skills, critical thinking, and social participation. For all the skills in each strand you are asked to identify the unit the skill is covered in, the date the unit will be taught, and how the skill will be assessed.

Social Studies Skills Checklist Grade 6, Page 19

This comprehensive checklist identifies grade level 6 social studies skills for 14 different strands including: history, geography, economics, culture, ethics and belief systems, social and political systems, national identity, constitutional heritage, citizenship, study skills, visual learning, map and globe skills, critical thinking, and social participation. For all the skills in each strand you are asked to identify the unit the skill is covered in, the date the unit will be taught, and how the skill will be assessed.

Social Studies Concept Development Checklist, Page 25

This comprehensive checklist can be invaluable to you as a "kidwatcher." It is convenient and quick to use and provides space for reporting on students each quarter. The following categories are included on the checklist: history, geography, citizenship, critical thinking, participation skills, and study skills. Several blank lines are provided for additional skills you would like to add.

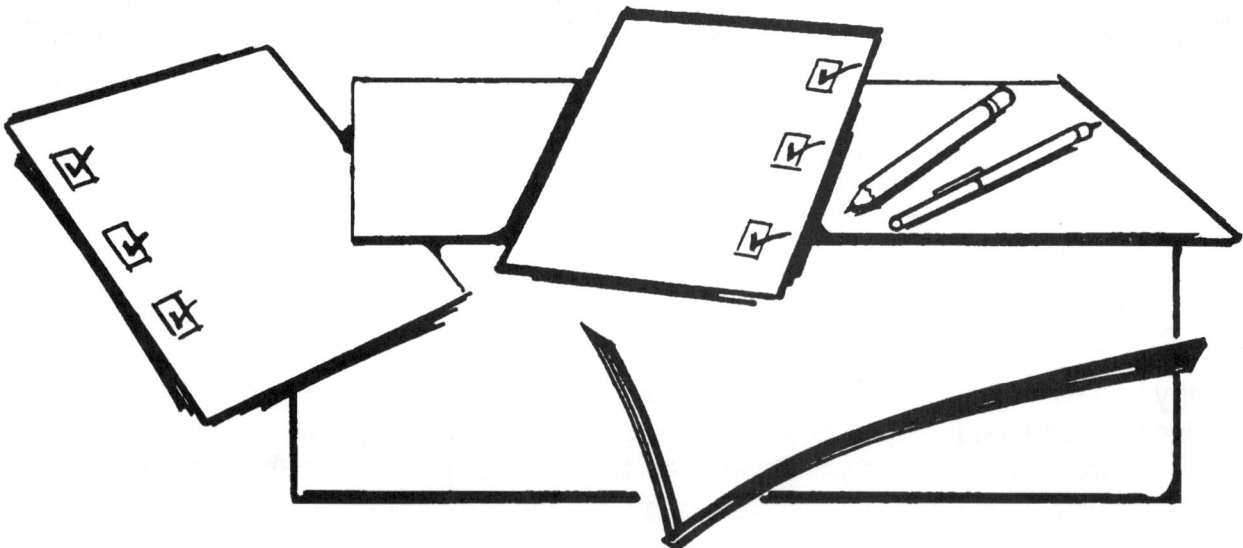

Social Studies Skills Checklist: Grade 5

Teacher's Name _____

School Year _____

Skill	Date	Unit	Form of Assessment
History			
Is aware of cultural heritage of self and others			
Knows historian's techniques			
Can use B.C./A.D.			
Can explain cause and effect of expansion			
Can explain cause and effect of wars			
Recognizes role of minorities in early societies			
Geography			
Is able to make historical analysis of places			
Recognizes use of natural resources			
Is aware of migration of people			
Compares/Contrasts regions over time			

Social Studies Skills Checklist Grade 5 *(cont.)*

Skill	Date	Unit	Form of Assessment
Economics			
Understands distribution of resources			
Knows about early exchange systems			
Recognizes role of trade routes			
Knows early economic history			
Realizes economic interdependence of states, nations			
Realizes impact of industrial revolution			
Culture			
Understands the role of education			
Understands the cultural complexity in the U.S.			
Recognizes contributions of minorities			
Understands interactions and conflicts on cultures			
Understands and appreciates cultural images			
Analyzes heroes/heroines			

Social Studies Skills Checklist Grade 5 *(cont.)*

Skill	Date	Unit	Form of Assessment
Ethics and Belief Systems			
Knows Pilgrims/Puritan's attitude on slavery			
Understands belief systems of Indians			
Understands belief systems of slaves			
Understands belief systems of immigrants			
Is aware of the freedom to dissent			
Social and Political Systems			
Recognizes early U.S. political systems			
Is aware of reinterpretation of law over time			
Identifies opposing ideals in early U.S. history			
Analyzes reasons for social structure change			
Identifies political systems of American Indians			
Identifies political systems of British			
Identifies political systems of French			
Identifies political systems of Spanish			
Understands relationship of U.S. with other countries			

Social Studies Skills Checklist Grade 5 *(cont.)*

Skill	Date	Unit	Form of Assessment
National Identity			
Knows about the origins of pluralism			
Knows the history of democracy in U.S.			
Recognizes American ideals and symbols			
Constitutional Heritage			
Understands checks and balances of power			
Knows about the writing of Constitution			
Knows about the passage of amendments			
Citizenship			
Understands the role of citizenship in U.S. history			
Can give examples of democratic behavior in history			
Knows the process for selection of leaders			
Is able to evaluate cases of human rights			
Knows about conflict resolution			
Recognizes crises in U.S. history			

Social Studies Skills Checklist Grade 5 *(cont.)*

Skill	Date	Unit	Form of Assessment
Study Skills			
Uses library catalog			
Interviews for information			
Uses oral discussion skills			
Plans reports			
Writes reports			
Visual Learning			
Makes line graphs			
Reads charts and tables			
Reads and uses diagrams			
Compares media			
Knows the history of national symbols			
Map and Globe Skills			
Understands parallels			
Understands meridians			
Uses latitude/longitude			
Traces explorers' routes			
Evaluates maps			
Draws maps			
Critical Thinking			
Asks appropriate questions			
Identifies fact/opinion			
Interprets cause/effect			
Draws conclusions			

Social Studies Skills Checklist Grade 5 (cont.)

Skill	Date	Unit	Form of Assessment
Social Participation			
Recognizes social needs of others			
Provides positive feedback			
Sets and plans goals			
Develops collaborative learning roles			
Other			

Social Studies Skills and Concepts Evaluation

Social Studies Skills Checklist Grade 6

Teacher's Name _____

School Year _____

Skill or Concept	Date	Unit	Form of Assessment
History			
Is aware of cultural heritage of self and others			
Knows historian's techniques			
Exhibits empathy for people of ancient times			
Understands cause/effect of territorial expansion			
Understands cultural diffusion			
Understands analysis of a civilization over time			
Recognizes the interrelatedness of trade and religion			
Is aware of women in ancient cultures			
Understands social classes in ancient cultures			
Geography			
Knows locations of cities			
Understands the influence of physical and cultural geography on civilizations			
Knows the origin of the city			
Recognizes environmental changes			
Knows about ancient migrations			
Identifies ancient trade routes			
Knows criteria to define regions			

Social Studies Skills Checklist Grade 6 *(cont.)*

Skill	Date	Unit	Form of Assessment
Economics			
Understands scarcity/specialization			
Knows early exchange systems			
Recognizes role of trade routes			
Understands ancient global trade			
Understands transportation changes			
Realizes effects of new technology			
Culture			
Defines culture			
Analyzes how culture is transmitted			
Analyzes prehistoric ancient cultures			
Identifies origins of contemporary cultures			
Analyzes interaction of cultures			
Analyzes conflict of cultures			
Understands and appreciates cultural images			
Knows myths in ancient cultures			

Social Studies Skills Checklist Grade 6 *(cont.)*

Skill	Date	Unit	Form of Assessment
Ethic and Belief Systems			
Makes comparisons of past societies			
Identifies belief systems of Buddhism			
Identifies belief systems of Judaism			
Identifies belief systems of Christianity			
Understands spread of religion through missionaries			
Knows early history of major religions			
Social and Political Systems			
Identifies social units in ancient times			
Identifies political units in ancient times			
Understands the origins of law			
Recognizes opposing ideals in ancient societies			
Understands social status in ancient times			
Understands interdependence in ancient times			

Social Studies Skills Checklist Grade 6 *(cont.)*

Skill	Date	Unit	Form of Assessment
National Identity			
Knows identities of ancient civilizations			
Knows origins of democracy in ancient times			
Identifies ancient national symbols			
Constitutional Heritage			
Understands balance of power in ancient times			
Citizenship			
Understands democratic behavior in ancient times			
Recognizes selection process of ancient leaders			
Is aware of minority rights long ago			
Knows about disputes in ancient times			
Understands pluralism in ancient times			
Understands why some past democracies failed			

Social Studies Skills Checklist Grade 6 *(cont.)*

Skill	Date	Unit	Form of Assessment
Study Skills			
Uses atlas			
Uses primary sources			
Identifies text patterns			
Uses oral discussion skills			
Plans reports			
Writes reports			
Visual Learning			
Makes telescoping time lines			
Makes parallel time lines			
Reads and makes graphic organizers			
Compares graphs			
Analyzes diagrams			
Interprets religious and historical symbols			
Makes a mural			
Map and Globe Skills			
Reads cartograms			
Draws inferences			
Uses latitude/longitude			
Formulates hypotheses			
Computes distances			
Computes travel time			
Makes a map			

Social Studies Skills Checklist Grade 6 *(cont.)*

Skill	Date	Unit	Form of Assessment
Critical Thinking			
Interprets values and ideologies			
Distinguishes fact/opinion/reasoned judgment			
Interprets cause/effect			
Draws conclusions			
Social Participation			
Recognizes social needs of others			
Provides positive feedback			
Sets and plans goals			
Develops collaborative learning roles			
Other			

Social Studies Concept Development Checklist

Student's Name _____ Grade _____

Rating Scale: 1 = Rarely Observed
2 = Occasionally Observed
3 = Often Observed

Concept				
History	**1**	**2**	**3**	**4**
Understands reasons for studying history				
Understands time lines/chronology				
Has a sense of empathy for the past				
Has an appreciation for our multicultural society				
Understands principles of democracy				
Appreciates American ideals				
Understands origins of Constitution and other historical documents				
Recognizes importance of religion in human society				
Is familiar with basic ideas of religion				
Understands conflict resolution				
Understands the role of laws				
Understands different political systems				
Geography	**1**	**2**	**3**	**4**
Uses locational skills				
Understands awareness of place				
Understands world regions				
Identifies and uses map and globe symbols				
Understands locational terms				
Understands directional terms				
Constructs maps				

Social Studies Concept Development *(cont.)*

Concept				
Citizenship	**1**	**2**	**3**	**4**
Understands duties of our leaders				
Understands voting procedures				
Has respect for human rights				
Understands responsibility of being a citizen in a democratic society				
Shows commitment to democratic values				
Critical Thinking Skills	**1**	**2**	**3**	**4**
Identifies central issues/problems				
Determines relevant information				
Distinguishes fact, opinion, and reasoned judgment				
Recognizes stereotypes, bias, and propaganda				
Analyzes cause/effect relationships				
Tests conclusions/hypotheses				
Justifies conclusions				
Identifies reasonable alternatives				
Predicts consequences of events				
Participation Skills	**1**	**2**	**3**	**4**
Expresses personal convictions				
Listens to differing points of view				
Formulates appropriate questions				
Recognizes personal bias				
Demonstrates skills of:				
persuasion				
compromise				
debate				
negotiation				

Social Studies Concept Development *(cont.)*

Concept				
Study Skills	**1**	**2**	**3**	**4**
Locates information				
Selects appropriate information				
Organizes information				
Acquires information by:				
listening				
observing				
locating community resources				
reading literature				
referring to primary sources				
Reads and interprets:				
maps				
globes				
models				
diagrams				
graphs				
charts				
time lines				
political cartoons				
Other	**1**	**2**	**3**	**4**

Getting Started_____

Rationale

As our philosophy and teaching methods for social studies change, we become aware of the need for a more authentic means of assessment. One such approach to process evaluation is the portfolio. Portfolios represent a philosophy that demands we view assessment as an integral part of instruction. It is an expanded definition of assessment in which a variety of indicators of learning are gathered across many situations. It is a philosophy that honors both the process and the products of learning as well as the active participation of the teacher and the students.

What will ultimately be included in the portfolio is up to you and your students. Suggestions include student work samples, self-evaluations, interest inventories, surveys, and anecdotal records.

How to Use Portfolios

The first step in beginning to use portfolios in your classroom is determining their purpose. The purpose will depend on the assessment needs in your classroom. Use the questions below to help you establish the purpose for the use of portfolios in your own classroom.

> ✐ Will the portfolio be a collection of work or a sample of the student's best work?
>
> ✐ Will the portfolio house finished products only?
>
> ✐ Will the portfolio be passed on to the next teacher?
>
> ✐ Who will select what is included in the portfolio?
>
> ✐ Who will have access to the portfolio?
>
> ✐ How will students be involved with the portfolio?

The next step is to consider where the portfolios will be housed. Depending on your purpose, you may or may not want students to have access to the portfolio. If the portfolio is exclusively for your own use, store it in a file cabinet to which students do not have access. On the other hand, if you want students to contribute to their portfolios, keep them in a highly visible place in the classroom. In either case, each student should have a clearly marked file folder to hold the contents of the portfolio. To help establish interest and ownership of the portfolio, allow students to decorate their portfolio folder any way they wish.

Getting Started *(cont.)*

Now that you have determined your purpose and set up the portfolio filing system, you must decide on what will be included in the portfolio. The possibilities are endless including student work samples, self-evaluations, interest inventories, surveys, and anecdotal records just to name a few. In this section of the resource guide you will find forms for students to record and evaluate their portfolio selections, an interest inventory, a social studies survey as well as a blank form to create your own, and three types of anecdotal record forms. However, all of the forms found in this assessment resource guide would be appropriate for the student's portfolio.

The final step in the portfolio process would be to decide how you will analyze the contents. Having an established criteria will greatly help you when report card time rolls around. You can use this criteria to review the contents of the portfolio and make a determination in regards to a formal grade, if your school requires that you give grades. Some schools are moving toward a narrative-type report card in which single grades give way to brief essays regarding student's progress. With this type of grading system, portfolios become an invaluable part of student assessment.

Using the Forms in This Section

Portfolio Activity Sample Cover Sheet, Page 32

If you allow students to take part in the selection process of the portfolio contents, this form can really come in handy. Students attach this form to the top of work samples they have selected for inclusion in their portfolios. On it they write the title of the assignment, why it was selected for the portfolio, and what they like best about their performance on the assignment.

Portfolio Record Keeping, Page 33

This form can be used by students to keep track of the assignments they have chosen for their portfolio for each unit of study. For each of four units of study, students are asked to choose three activities for inclusion in their portfolio as well as selecting which was their favorite activity.

Getting Started *(cont.)*

Portfolio Content Analysis, Page 34

After all portfolio items have been collected you will want to analyze the students' progress. This narrative form allows you to make notes regarding a student's performance on classroom work, research projects, cooperative investigations, written products, and self evaluations. This information can then be transferred to a narrative report card, comment section of a traditional report card, or used as concrete data to support report card grades during parent conferences.

Interest Inventory, Page 35

Interest inventories allow teachers to find out basic personal information about students' likes, dislikes, hobbies, and friends. Interest inventories can be particularly valuable at the beginning of the year when you are trying to get to know each of your students. The information provided can help you to plan thematic units based on topics in which your students are interested.

Social Studies Survey, Page 36

Surveys are also valuable at the beginning of the year. However, if you use surveys over time, say at the beginning of the year and then again several months later, you may notice changing attitudes and interests that can again help in curriculum planning. Use this survey to find out about students' attitudes toward the study of history. Find out what they enjoy about the subject and what frustrates them. With this survey you can also find out if students understand the importance of studying the past.

Student Survey, Page 37

This blank form can be used to create your own survey on a topic of your choice. There is room for you to write or type in five different questions for students to answer. Below is an example of survey questions.

1. What is your opinion of war?

2. Would you like to learn about the Civil War?

3. What do you already know about the Civil War?

4. What would you like to know about the Civil War?

5. What projects could we do related to the Civil War?

Getting Started *(cont.)*

Anecdotal Record Form #1, Page 38

Anecdotal notes and observations are carefully documented records of certain events, behaviors, and skills. It provides a record that you can review independently or share with parents during conference time. When these notes and observations are put together they tell an on-going story about the student's growth and progress. This form can be used to record information about a single student about a specific event. The first three observations are objective, simply asking you to record information. The final question asks you to be interpretive and identify why the behavior is important.

Anecdotal Record Form #2, Page 39

This form can also be used to record information on a single student but it has space to note several observations. Because you can record several events on this single sheet, it is important to date your observations.

Anecdotal Record Form #3, Page 40

This anecdotal record form can be used to record information about all students in your class. Again, it is important to note the date of your observations. This form is both objective and interpretive in that it asks for a description of the incident and also its possible implications.

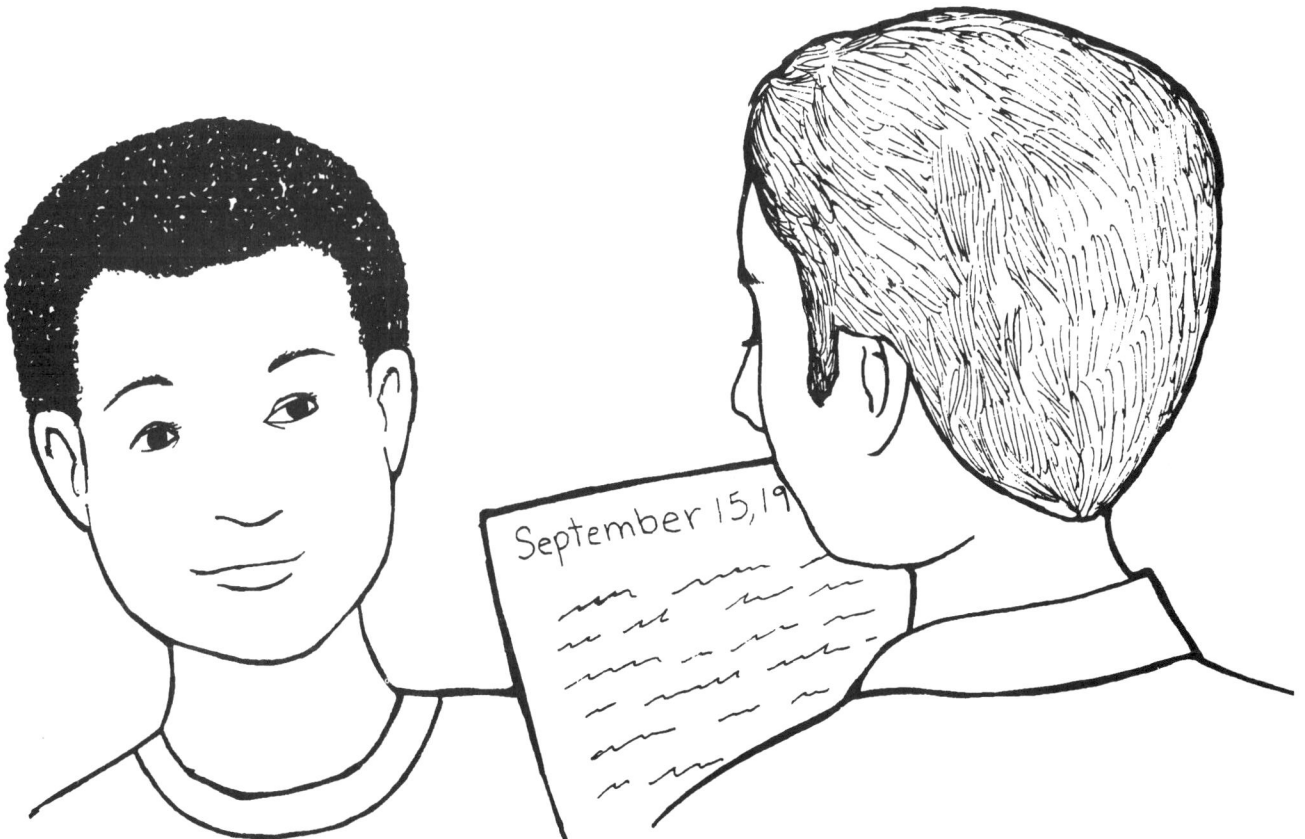

Portfolio Activity Sample Cover Sheet

Name _____

Date _____

Title of the assignment:

_____

Why did you choose this assignment for your portfolio?

_____

_____

_____

_____

_____

What do you like best about your performance on this assignment?

_____

_____

_____

_____

_____

32

Portfolio Record Keeping

Name _____

Date

_____ Unit One _____

_____ Activity 1 _____

_____ Activity 2 _____

_____ Activity 3 _____

My favorite activity was: _____

_____ Unit Two _____

_____ Activity 1 _____

_____ Activity 2 _____

_____ Activity 3 _____

My favorite activity was: _____

_____ Unit Three _____

_____ Activity 1 _____

_____ Activity 2 _____

_____ Activity 3 _____

My favorite activity was: _____

_____ Unit Four _____

_____ Activity 1 _____

_____ Activity 2 _____

_____ Activity 3 _____

My favorite activity was: _____

Portfolio Content Analysis

Student's Name _____ Date _____

Classroom Work:

Research Projects:

Cooperative Investigations:

Written Products:

Self-Evaluations:

Interest Inventory

Name _____ Date_____

1. What is your favorite subject in school? _____

2. What is your least favorite subject in school? _____

3. What do you like to do in your free time? _____

    _____

4. Who is your best friend? _____

5. What is your favorite sport? _____

6. What is your favorite animal? _____

7. Name something you do very well. _____

    _____

8. Name something that makes you mad. _____

    _____

9. What is your favorite T.V. show? _____

10. What is your favorite book? _____

11. What is your favorite movie? _____

12. If you could meet a famous person, who would it be?_____

13. Why would you like to meet that person? _____

    _____

14. What would you like to be when you grow-up? _____

    _____

15. What would you like to learn in school this year? _____

    _____

Social Studies Survey

Name _____ Date _____

1. How do you feel about studying social studies? _____

   _____

   _____

2. Is it important to know about the past? _____

   _____

3. Is it important to know about other people and cultures? _____

   _____

4. What do you enjoy about the study of history? _____

   _____

   _____

5. What do you find frustrating about the study of history? _____

   _____

   _____

6. What would you like to learn about in social studies this year? _____

   _____

   _____

Student Survey

Name _____	Date _____

1. _____

   _____

   _____

2. _____

   _____

   _____

3. _____

   _____

   _____

4. _____

   _____

   _____

5. _____

   _____

   _____

Anecdotal Record Form #1

Student's Name _____

Date _____

Subject _____

Instructional Situation	
Instructional Task	
Behavior Observed	
This behavior was important because	

Anecdotal Record Form #2

Student's Name _____

Date	Observation	Watch for

Anecdotal Record Form #3

Name	Date	Activity	Implication

Getting Started_____

Rationale

In order to enhance student understanding of historical events, and provide motivation for learning about the event, students should be encouraged to read a historical novel for each unit of study. Now that there is such an abundant selection of historical literature available, students can be allowed to self-select the novel they will read. However, if we allow students to select their own books to read, how do we keep track of their progress? Student logs and journals can be an excellent way of charting student work, progress, and attitude for self-selected novels, and for whole class studies of particular novels.

Reading logs are designed to track progress and time spent reading during a specified period of time. The time limit is set at your discretion and may include the time spent during a particular unit of study, or simple tracking by month.

A journal is one step beyond a log. In the journal students are asked to respond to the books they are reading rather than just keeping a list of the titles. By reading the student's journal you can get a good idea of not only their reading comprehension ability, but also their ability to communicate in writing and understand historical concepts. The motivation for keeping the journal is the personal response you write back to the student. When teachers and students write back and forth to each other a more personal relationship can develop. With class sizes constantly increasing, the journal may be the only opportunity for the teacher and student to have a one-to-one correspondence on a regular basis. Students will undoubtedly enjoy this special attention.

How to Use Logs and Journals

The log is simple to use and merely requires that the student record what he/she has read during a period of time. The reading log included in this guide is for a one month period, but you can adjust that if you wish.

As was said earlier, journals have a more complex purpose. After reading a story on their own, or as a class, you may ask the students to respond to the story in their journal. You may wish to ask students to respond to the questions below. Other suggestions are provided in the "Literature Response Guide" on page 46.

☞ What was the story about?

☞ Do you remember any of the details of the story?

☞ Where did the story take place?

☞ During what time period did the story take place?

☞ Who were the people in the story?

☞ Did you like the story?

☞ Was the story historically accurate?

Getting Started *(cont.)* _____

After the student has responded to the story in the journal it is important that you read the response and write back. This provides the motivation for the student to continue journal writing. After the student has several responses in the journal you can begin the evaluation process. Read the responses and then use the "Reading Journal Evaluation" form on page 48 to assist you in the assessment process. One final note, it may be important for you to stress the confidentiality of logs and journals to students. They will often write personal responses and should therefore feel assured that you will be the only one to read it.

Using the Forms in This Section

Monthly Reading Log, Page 44

Use this form to help students track their independent reading of historical fiction and nonfiction during a one month period. By encouraging students to complete this form, you will gain a better idea of their use of independent time in class.

Book Review Form, Page 45

This book review form allows the student the opportunity to become a book critic. They are asked why they chose the book and to briefly summarize the story. Then, they are asked to rate the book, as well as justifying that rating. Finally, they are asked if the book was historically accurate which is very important in making the connections between the literature and social studies and history concepts.

Literature Response Guide, Page 46

Students can be given this guide to assist them in writing quality literature responses for their journals. The first step asks the students to summarize with details. Then, there are nine questions that require students to react to the story.

42

Getting Started *(cont.)*_____

Dialectical Journal, Page 47

This double entry journal asks students to note and respond to text in the novel that was powerful to them. It may be for historical reasons, or it may be for personal reasons that a bit of text had special meaning to the student. The importance of this journal is that students decide what is powerful based on their own background and experiences. Again, as with other journals, your personal response back to the student is both motivating and appreciated.

Reading Journal Evaluation, Page 48

If you ask students to keep a journal of their responses to books read, you will need a way to assess these responses. The "Reading Journal Evaluation" is an excellent way of reviewing what the students have written and determining their level of comprehension. The evaluation also considers their ability to communicate in writing and understanding of historical concepts.

Facts and Feelings Chart, Page 49

This chart is particularly important in helping students make the connection between facts in the history textbook and feelings in historical novels. The fact portion of this chart is completed by students as they read their textbook. The feelings/reactions portion of the chart is completed as students read the novel about that time period. Understanding feelings and reactions to historical events helps make the events more real to students rather than just "something that happened a long time ago." It also helps students to realize consequences and repercussions of historical events that they may not understand by simply reading the textbook.

Monthly Reading Log

Use this form to record all the reading you do in one month.

Name _____

Month _____

Title of Book	Author	Historical Topic	Pages	Comments

What was your favorite book of the month? _____

_____

What was the best part of the book? _____

_____

What do you plan to read next month? _____

_____

Book Review Form

Name _____

Title of book _____

Author _____

Number of pages _____

Historical topic _____

1. Why did you choose this book? _____

_____

_____

2. Summarize the story. _____

_____

_____

_____

3. How do you rate this book?
   _____ Exciting
   _____ Interesting
   _____ O.K.
   _____ Dull

4. Why did you give the book that rating? _____

_____

5. Was the book historically accurate? Give examples. _____

_____

_____

_____

_____

Reviewer's signature _____

Literature Response Guide

Name _____ Date _____

Use this guide to assist you in literature response journal writing.

Step One

Summary:

Summarize the story in your own words including details on characters, main events, setting, historical time period, climax, and resolution.

Step Two

Your Reactions:

1. How did the main character feel when faced with a conflict?

2. Why did the character react the way he or she did?

3. Should the character have acted that way?

4. What would you have done?

5. What does the story remind you of?

6. What did you like about the book?

7. What did you dislike about the book?

8. If you were the writer, what would you change?

9. Did the author make you feel that you were transported to that particular time in history?

Dialectical Journal

Name _____

Book _____

Text	Response

Reading Journal Evaluation

Student's Name _____

Date of Evaluation _____

Number of Entries _____

1. Can the reader communicate in writing? _____

   Examples: _____

   _____

   _____

2. Can the reader recall details about the story? _____

   Examples: _____

   _____

   _____

3. Does the reader appear to understand story elements such as setting, character, and plot?

   Examples: _____

   _____

   _____

4. Does the reader give substantiated opinions of the story?

   Examples: _____

   _____

   _____

5. Does the reader understand the historical concepts?

   Examples: _____

   _____

   _____

   Other observations: _____

   _____

Facts and Feelings Chart

Name _____

Unit of Study _____

Historical Novel _____

Historical Facts	Character Feelings/Reactions

Getting Started

Rationale

Performance assessment is a means to evaluate students in a variety of contexts by allowing them to demonstrate their understanding of concepts and apply knowledge and skills they have acquired. Performance assessment tasks are carefully constructed in order to assess specific declarative and procedural knowledge as well as critical thinking skills. Declarative knowledge refers to facts about certain persons, places, and things, and generalizations or concepts that can be derived based on those facts. Procedural knowledge refers to skills and strategies. The tasks used to assess this knowledge are scored based on grading rubrics that are, in most cases, established by the teacher prior to introducing the task.

A rubric is a set of criteria the student sees prior to engaging in the performance task. The rubric identifies the qualities the teacher expects to see in a response at several points along a scale. By establishing the criteria prior to the activity the student clearly knows what is expected in order to receive a specific score. Each score on the rubric is matched to an example of a response.

A rubric can be used in two ways: as an assessment tool and as a teaching tool. When a rubric is used as an assessment tool it serves as a standard against which a sample of student work can be measured. When a rubric is used as a teaching tool it provides an example for students to follow and can actually promote learning by offering clear performance standards for students.

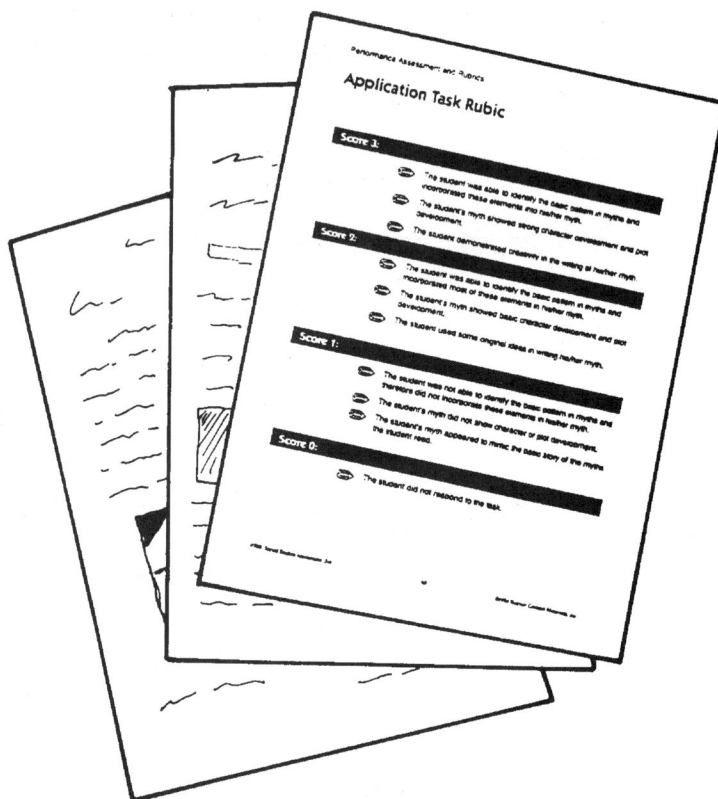

How to Use Performance Assessments and Rubrics

The construction of a performance task can be a time consuming process. However, with practice the tasks become easier to write. An added benefit is that the tasks can be used from one year to the next so you will not have to recreate a whole new set of tasks each school year.

Getting Started *(cont.)* _____

The first step in creating a performance task is to determine what content knowledge you wish to assess. Then you should determine if this content knowledge is declarative or procedural. If you are assessing declarative knowledge your task should require students to respond in some fashion to a generalization. Students will then respond to this generalization according to the task using their knowledge of basic facts. If you are assessing procedural knowledge, students should be required to apply a strategy such as a problem solving strategy. In their application of this strategy they must naturally apply their knowledge of basic skills. Also consider what critical thinking skills students will have to use in order to complete the performance task.

Once you have made all the important decisions about knowledge to assess you can write the task. Like any other piece of writing it may take several drafts before you are completely satisfied. You should also include in the task the way in which the students will present their findings or answer. Some presentation ideas may include a written report, a letter to an official, a debate, or a videotape.

Once you have completed writing the task you must develop a rubric to score student responses. At this level you may wish to have three to four categories of performance standards on your rubric. There are many examples of performance tasks and rubrics in this resource guide to assist you in the development process specifically a comparison task, an application task, and an analyzing perspectives task.

The task and the rubric should be established and discussed clearly with students prior to the activity. Keep in mind that the burden of establishing criteria does not always have to rest upon the teacher. Students' opinions can be solicited prior to establishing the rubric. A blank rubric form has been included in this resource guide for you to use when allowing students to participate in the rubric development process. By assisting in the creation of a rubric, students may become more aware of task expectations and may therefore perform better.

Getting Started *(cont.)*

Using the Forms in This Section

Performance Task Types and Descriptions, Page 54

This page describes twelve types of performance assessment tasks that can be used to evaluate students in social studies. Examples of three of these performance assessments are included in this section of the resource guide.

Comparison Task, Page 55

This performance task asks students to compare pioneer life with modern life and identify similarities and differences. Background information is provided along with an excerpt from Laura Ingalls Wilder's *The Long Winter* to provide even more information to students. Then, students are asked to write an essay describing the ways in which pioneer life and modern life are the same and different. The task is described for the students in detail.

Comparison Task Venn Diagram, Page 56

This activity sheet can be used by students to help them perform the comparison task described on page 55.

Comparison Task Rubric, Page 57

As described earlier, for every performance task a rubric is needed in order to score the student's product. This rubric is specifically written for the performance task on page 55.

Application Task, Page 58

The second example of performance assessment asks students to apply their knowledge to a new situation. The subject of this task is Greek myths. Background information on Greek gods, along with a list of several Greek gods, is provided for students. Students are asked to read three myths and then write their own myth based on the pattern they discovered while reading the myths on their own. This task is described for students in great detail.

Application Task Pre-Writing Activity Sheet, Page 59

This page will assist students in gathering their ideas prior to writing their own Greek myth as described on page 58.

Application Task Rubric, Page 60

This rubric is specifically designed for the application performance task on page 58.

Getting Started (cont.)

Analyzing Perspectives Task, Page 61

This performance task asks students to analyze two different perspectives on rain forest destruction and then to determine which perspective they agree with. Information on the Amazon rain forest is provided along with the perspectives of environmental activists and Brazilians. Students are asked to write a position statement expressing their opinion. The task is described for students in detail.

Analyzing Perspectives Task Visual Representation, Page 62

This activity sheet will help students visually represent the two perspectives on rain forest destruction and the motivations behind the perspectives. This will make it easier for students to determine their own opinion on the issue.

Analyzing Perspectives Task Rubric, Page 63

This rubric was specifically designed for the Analyzing Perspectives Task on page 61.

Create a Task, Page 64

Using the theoretical information provided in the "Getting Started" portion of this section and the examples of performance assessment provided you can create your own performance assessment task for a specific unit your students are studying. This blank is just like the examples provided for ease and convenience.

Create a Rubric, Page 65

If you create your own performance assessment task you will also need to create your own rubric. This page is just like the rubric pages used in the examples for ease and convenience.

Performance Task Recording Sheet, Page 66

This sheet can be used to record student grades on each of the 12 types of performance assessment tasks.

Individual Student Performance Task Recording Sheet, Page 67

This narrative record sheet can be used to record the strengths and weaknesses on a performance task for an individual student. There is also space to make notes about what you would like to specifically work on with that student to improve his or her performance.

Performance Task Types and Descriptions

Comparison Task: The student is required to compare two or more people, places, or things.

Classification Task: The student is asked to classify, or put into categories, certain people, places, or things.

Position Support Task: The student is asked to take a position on a subject or issue and defend that position.

Application Task: The student is asked to apply their knowledge in a new situation.

Analyzing Perspectives Task: The student is asked to analyze two to three different perspectives and then choose the perspective they support.

Decision Making Task: The student must identify the factors that caused a certain decision to be made.

Historical Perspective Task: The student must consider differing theories to answer basic historical questions.

Predictive Task: The student must make predictions about what could have happened or will happen in the future.

Problem Solving Task: The student must create a solution to a specific problem.

Experimental Task: The student sets up an experiment to test a hypothesis.

Invention Task: The student must create something new and unique.

Error Identification Task: The student must identify specific errors.

Comparison Task

Background Information:

Even before America won its independence, settlers were pushing west of the Appalachian Mountains. There was adventure and opportunity in these new lands that many could not resist. However, the trip west was no easy task. Early pioneers braved rough roads and dangerous rivers, the blistering heat of the summer and unbearable cold of the winter. Even when the pioneers found a place to settle they still struggled. The life and struggles of pioneers has been beautifully chronicled in Laura Ingalls Wilder's Little House Series.

An Excerpt from *The Long Winter* by Laura Ingalls Wilder (Harper Collins, 1968)

Winter had lasted so long that it seemed it would never end. It seemed that they would never really wake up. In the morning Laura got out of bed into the cold. She dressed downstairs by the fire that Pa had kindled before he went to the stable. They ate their coarse brown bread. Then all day long she and Ma and Mary ground wheat and twisted hay as fast as they could. The fire must not go out; it was very cold. They ate some coarse brown bread. Then Laura crawled into the cold bed and shivered until she grew warm enough to sleep.

Next morning she got out of bed into the cold. She dressed in the chilly kitchen by the fire. She ate her coarse brown bread. She took her turns at grinding wheat and twisting hay. But she did not ever feel awake. She felt beaten by the cold and the storms. She knew she was dull and stupid but she could not wake up.

Your Task:

You have just read a short excerpt from *The Long Winter*. To fully understand what Laura and her family went through as early pioneers, you should read the entire novel. While reading the novel, note differences between life on the frontier and your own life. Use the chart and Venn diagram on the following page to help you organize the information you gather. Then, write an essay about the ways in which pioneer life and modern life are the same and also the ways in which they are different.

Comparison Task

Venn Diagram

Name_____ Date _____

Characteristics of Pioneer Life	Characteristics of Modern Life

In the outer portions of the circles list items the two ways of life do not have in common. In the center, overlapping portion of the circles, list items the two ways of life have in common.

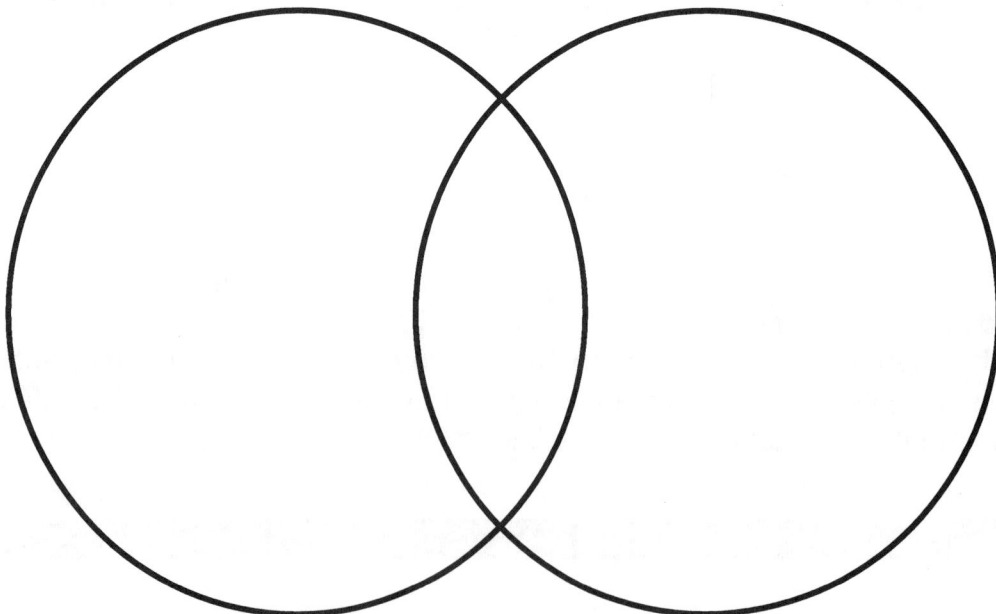

Comparison Task Rubric

Score 3:

☞ The student read the novel and identified most of the ways in which pioneer life is the same and different from modern life.

☞ The student's essay clearly expressed the most dramatic ways in which pioneer life is the same and different from modern life.

Score 2:

☞ The student read the novel and identified many of the ways in which pioneer life is the same and different from modern life.

☞ The student's essay expresses many of the ways in which pioneer life is the same and different from modern life.

Score 1:

The student read the novel, but identified only a few ways in which pioneer life is the same and different from modern life.

The student's essay expressed few ways in which pioneer life is the same and different from modern life.

Score 0:

The student did not respond to the task.

Application Task

Background Information:

The Olympic games originally began in Ancient Greece in 776 B.C. Foot races were a popular Olympic event and Coroebus, a cook, was the first recorded winner at the Olympic games. Modern day Olympics are modeled after these Greek games.

The Greeks considered the Olympics an important sporting event, but it was also a time to honor the gods. Zeus was honored at the Olympics. He was thought to be the master of the entire world and portrayed as powerful, stern, and commanding. The Greeks believed that Zeus controlled the weather and punished wrongdoing with lightening and thunder.

Zeus was not the only powerful god. The Greeks believed that the gods controlled all natural phenomenon. For example, Apollo controlled the movement of the sun across the sky each day.

Other Greek Gods:

Poseidon	Hera	Ares
Minerva	Daphne	Cupid
Aphrodite	Athena	Hermes

Your Task:

You need to choose three Greek myths about powerful gods that you would like to read. A good resource for myths is *Favorite Greek Myths* by Mary Pope Osborne (Scholastic, 1989). As you read the myths look for common patterns in the stories. Your task is to write an original myth about a fictitious Greek god using the same general pattern as the myths you read. Use the pre-writing questions on the following page to help you organize your thoughts prior to writing your myth. Your story will become part of a class book of original Greek myths.

Application Task
Pre-Writing Activity Sheet

Name _____ Date _____

Which fictitious god will you write your myth about? _____

_____

What is the god's official title? _____

Who are the god's parents? _____

What special powers does the god have? _____

_____

What animals or objects are sacred to the god? _____

_____

_____

Where will your myth take place? _____

Who will the other characters be? _____

_____

_____

What will be the basic plot of your myth? _____

_____

_____

_____

_____

_____

Application Task Rubic

Score 3:

✎ The student was able to identify the basic pattern in myths and incorporated these elements into his/her myth.

✎ The student's myth showed strong character development and plot development.

✎ The student demonstrated creativity in the writing of his/her myth.

Score 2:

✎ The student was able to identify the basic pattern in myths and incorporated most of these elements in his/her myth.

✎ The student's myth showed basic character development and plot development.

✎ The student used some original ideas in writing his/her myth.

Score 1:

✎ The student was not able to identify the basic pattern in myths and therefore did not incorporate these elements in his/her myth.

✎ The student's myth did not show character or plot development.

✎ The student's myth appeared to mimic the basic story of the myths the student read.

Score 0:

✎ The student did not respond to the task.

Analyzing Perspectives Task

Background Information:

Rain forest destruction has become big news in recent years. Many people worry about the future of the Amazon rain forest in Brazil if deforestation is allowed to continue there. Brazilians living in this rapidly diminishing country are concerned with their country's economic well being.

Differing Perspectives:

The United States has many powerful environmental activist groups that are sincerely concerned about rain forest destruction. According to some estimates, every second of every day we are losing a tropical forest the size of a football field. Activists contend that when forests go, so do animals, plants, insects, and birds.

Brazilians have a different perspective on the same issue. Brazil has a large and rapidly growing population. Providing jobs for this large population is paramount to the country's economic well being. Brazil's exports include cattle and lumber. Forests are cleared so that cattle can graze and to provide lumber to export. The use of the rain forest is necessary to raise the standard of living of Brazilians.

Your Task:

You have been provided with two different perspectives regarding the Amazon rain forest in Brazil. Consider the motivations behind each of the two perspectives such as economic motivation, emotional motivation, and cultural motivation. Use the visual representation sheet to help you organize this information. Your responses on this chart will be used to determine part of your grade on this task. After you have analyzed the perspectives determine your own position on this issue. Write a position statement presenting your opinion, what information you have based that opinion on, and what specifically made you choose that opinion.

Analyzing Perspectives Task: Visual Representation

Name _____

Date _____

	Environmental Activist	Brazilian
Position on rain forest issue		
Motivation for position on rain forest		

Your opinion: _____

_____

_____

_____

_____

_____

_____

_____

_____

Analyzing Perspectives Task Rubric

Score 3:

- The student clearly identifies the two positions on rain forests.

- The student clearly understands the motivations behind the two positions both explicit and implicit.

- The student clearly articulates his/her view on the rain forest issue with a strong line of reasoning to support it.

Score 2:

- The student has a basic understanding of the two rain forest perspectives.

- The student has a basic understanding of the motivations behind the two perspectives.

- The student articulates his/her view on the rain forest, but with little support.

Score 1:

- The student did not have a basic understanding of the two perspectives or their motivations.

- The student did not clearly articulate his/her opinion of the rain forest issue.

Score 0:

- The student did not respond to the task.

Create a Task

Background Information:

Other Information:

Your Task:

64

Create a Rubric

Type of task _____

Score 3:

Score 2:

Score 1:

Score 0:

Performance Task Recording Sheet

Student	Comparison Task	Classification Task	Position Support Task	Application Task	Analyzing Perspectives Task	Decision-Making Task	Historical Perspective Task	Predictive Task	Problem-Solving Task	Experimental Task	Invention Task	Error Analysis Task

66

Individual Student Performance Task Recording Sheet

Student's Name _____

Date _____ Grade Level _____

Type of Performance Task _____

Description of Task:

Student's Strengths:

Student's Weaknesses:

Assist student with:

Getting Started

Rationale

Cooperative investigations in social studies require students to work in heterogeneous groups toward a common goal of a particular task. Cooperative investigations encourage students to become partners in learning rather than competitors. Working in heterogeneous groups allows students to learn both with each other and from each other.

In cooperative investigations each student has a particular job or responsibility to the group. Therefore, each student must make a contribution in order to successfully complete the task. It is important that students develop the skills necessary for working with others in groups. Research shows that these skills are valuable later in life as students become working adults.

How to Use Cooperative Investigations

Cooperative investigations must be structured so that all students have an important role in the completion of the task. It is also important that groups are heterogeneously organized, not organized according to ability. The best group size at the 5th and 6th grade level is about four to five students. Groups should also be gender and racially balanced as much as possible.

Once you have determined the participants in each group, you can assign them their roles. Five basic roles are described below:

Reader: Reads all directions and sees that they are followed.

Recorder: Writes group answers.

Manager: Divides up the group work and keeps everyone on task.

Leader: Leads discussions and keeps everyone involved.

Monitor: Watches time, hands out materials, paper, and supplies. (This is an optional role.)

68

Getting Started *(cont.)* _____

Students within the groups as well as the teacher can evaluate the effectiveness of each group member in relation to the completion of the assigned task.

This section will include examples of three types of cooperative investigations. The first is a general group task and can be found on page 71. In this cooperative investigation students work cooperatively to solve a problem related to going west on a wagon.

The second investigation included in this guide is a "jigsaw" activity. The example can be found on page 72. In a jigsaw each student becomes an expert on a particular topic that is related to a larger project. Then the student shares that knowledge with his or her "home" group. To organize a jigsaw activity you first need to identify several topics that are related to a larger topic or concept. Then set up an "expert" group for each smaller topic made up of one member from each "home" team. The "expert" group works together to research their topic. "Experts" then return to their "home" teams to share the fruits of their research with the others. The "home" teams then complete a final project such as a paper or oral presentation. The jigsaw activity in this resource guide relates to solving community dilemmas.

The third type of cooperative investigation included in this guide is simulations. Simulations get students actively involved in history by participating in problem-solving dilemmas relating to causes and implications of historical events. The simulation places the student in the middle of a situation relevant to a famous episode in history. An example of a simulation can be found on page 73. It requires students to take part in a mock trial.

Using the Forms in This Section

General Group Task: Pioneers, Page 71

This is an example of a general group task that requires all students in the group to actively participate in a common goal. This example asks students to decide what items they would choose to take with them if they were part of a wagon train moving west.

Jigsaw Cooperative Task: Solving Community Dilemmas, Page 72

In this example students must become experts on a particular community problem. After reporting the research on their community problem to their "home" group, the group selects one problem for which to try to find a solution.

Getting Started (cont.)

Simulation Task: Mock Trial, Page 73

This simulation asks students to take part in a mock trial of six Athenian navy generals.

Group Process Evaluation, Page 74

This form allows each participant in the group to evaluate the group's overall performance on the cooperative investigation task. Students are also asked to describe the group's strengths and frustrations, and to identify two ways in which the group could improve their effectiveness.

Cooperative Learning Peer Evaluation, Page 75

This form allows students to evaluate the performance of each member of their group on their particular task in the cooperative investigation. Students are asked to rate each member of the group as effective or ineffective and to provide supporting comments as well. This form can also be used by the teacher.

Teacher Evaluation of Cooperative Groups, Page 76

As you observe the cooperative groups in action you can assess their effectiveness by completing this evaluation form. You are asked to observe how decisions are made, if the students were helping each other, if it was necessary for you to intervene, and if the group met their task objective. There is additional room provided for you to comment on individual members of the group.

General Group Task: Pioneers

Name _____

Members of your group _____

Imagine that you are about to embark upon a long journey west. Because you are limited in the amount of supplies that you can take on the wagon, you must prioritize your list of supplies and choose some things to leave behind. Below is a list of items you need to choose from when deciding what you will take with you on your wagon. First, choose items yourself. Then, meet in your group to discuss everyone's choices. Because you will all be traveling together, your group must reach consensus on what items you should take and what should be left behind. Make a final list to include the items your group chose to take. Your final list may include only 10 items.

Individual Ranking	Group Consensus	Items
_____	_____	Box of matches
_____	_____	50 feet of rope
_____	_____	Ax
_____	_____	5 gallons of water
_____	_____	Rifle
_____	_____	Extra moccasins
_____	_____	Shovel
_____	_____	5 lbs. of salt
_____	_____	5 lbs. of sugar
_____	_____	Seeds for crops
_____	_____	Cornmeal
_____	_____	Dried meat
_____	_____	Coffee
_____	_____	5 gallons of milk
_____	_____	Dried fruit
_____	_____	One toy for child
_____	_____	Fresh meat

Jigsaw Task:
Solving Community Dilemmas

Name _____

Members of "home" group _____

Members of "expert" group_____

In each community in the United States there are problems that the citizens face. The challenge lies in trying to fully understand the complexities of the problem and then devising a feasible solution. You, along with the members of your "expert" group will become well versed on a particular problem your community faces. You will need to research the problem by locating newspaper articles and community newsletters and interviewing people within your community. Your "expert" group must become knowledgeable enough about the community problem for each of you to be able to explain the problem in detail to your "home" group.

When you meet with your "home" group explain what you learned about the problem your "expert" group studied. When all members of the "home" group have had the opportunity to explain what they know about their community problem, the "home" group as a whole should choose just one problem to tackle finding a solution for.

Your "home" group will devise a feasible plan to solve the community problem you chose. Then, you will write a letter to a local government official describing your recommendations for solving the problem.

Sample community problems:

homelessness	lack of community services
lack of recycling	graffiti
gang activity	litter

Simulation Task:
Mock Trial

As long ago as 700 B.C. Athenians were holding trials similar to those we have today. The Athenians developed a form of government that put decision making power into the hands of the people. This form of government is known as "democracy." In a democracy, citizens have a right to a trial to prove their innocence.

A story has been told about six Athenian navy generals who were accused of abandoning hundreds of shipwrecked soldiers and leaving them to drown. Their guilt was decided by a jury of some 2,000 Athenian citizens.

Your simulation involves conducting a mock trial of those six Athenian navy generals. Here are the basic contentions of the accused and the witnesses:

Generals: They did all they could to save the lives of the men.

Witness #1: The generals were only concerned with saving themselves and did not attempt to help any of the others.

Witness #2: The generals did all they could to save the lives of the men.

Students need to be selected for the following roles:

Six Athenian navy generals
Lawyer for the defense
Witness #1
Witness #2
Lawyer for the prosecution
Jury (an appropriate number)
Judge
Public Crier (advises the jury)
Observers

Stage the trial and allow the jury to decide the guilt or innocence of the generals.

Group Process Evaluation

Name _____

Group Members _____

Cooperative Task _____

_____

1. Describe the effectiveness of your group on the task. _____

_____

_____

_____

2. What were the group's strengths? _____

_____

_____

_____

3. What frustrations did the group encounter? _____

_____

_____

_____

4. Did all members of the group participate? _____

5. Did you listen to each other? _____

6. Name two ways in which your group could improve in order to be more effective on your next cooperative task.

    a. _____

      _____

    b. _____

      _____

Cooperative Learning Peer Evaluation

Name _____

Group Members _____

Cooperative Task _____

_____

Role	Effective	Ineffective	Comments
Reader			
Recorder			
Manager			
Leader			
Monitor			

Teacher Evaluation of Cooperative Groups

Cooperative task _____

Date_____

Number of students in the group _____

Members of the group _____

_____

1. How were decisions made? _____

_____

_____

2. How did students help each other achieve a common goal? _____

_____

_____

3. Did you have to intervene at any time? If so, why? _____

_____

_____

4 Did the group meet the cooperative investigation objective? _____

Evidence or examples: _____

_____

_____

_____

_____

Comments on individual group members:

_____

_____

_____

_____

76   ©1994 Teacher Created Materials, Inc.

Getting Started

Rationale

Research projects give students the opportunity to study one topic for an extended period of time. Because students have the opportunity to focus on the single topic they gain a much deeper understanding. In conducting the necessary research for their project students practice important study and library skills such as getting the main idea, drawing conclusions, note taking, and the use of library reference materials.

Not all research projects have to be long term. Students can do minimal research projects focusing on current events. Most teachers have a specified time during the week in which students are asked to report on current events as part of the social studies curriculum. If students are given certain topics such as world events, community news, or sports they can conduct a minimal bit of research just using their daily newspaper. Now students are learning basic research skills and becoming familiar with the organization of a newspaper.

One of the many benefits of assigning research projects to students is the way in which oral communication skills can be integrated. Students can be asked to make an oral presentation following the completion of a long term research project to report their findings to the rest of the class. Or, students can be asked to present their current event news to the class. Either way students are practicing their public speaking skills which are clearly very important.

How to Use Research Projects

Probably the most difficult skill for students to master when doing long term research projects is time management. The "Independent Research Contract" included in this section on page 79 can help students better manage their time for the project.

It will also be necessary to train students on oral presentation skills. You may need to model appropriate public speaking skills by making a formal presentation to the class yourself. It may also be helpful if students were given a copy of the "Oral Presentation Evaluation" form on page 83. This way students will know what you are looking for when assessing their oral presentations.

Getting Started *(cont.)* _____

Using the Forms in This Section

Independent Research Contract, Page 79

This form can be used to help students better manage their time for the long term research project. Students are asked what they need to know and how they will go about obtaining that information. They are also asked to provide a time line to which you should strongly encourage them to stick. Finally students are asked how they will present their findings.

Research Project Cover Sheet, Page 80

This cover sheet is used to accompany the final draft of the student's research project. On it they are required to note their effectiveness in gathering information and communicating it in the report. They are also asked to consider what they will focus on in their oral presentation.

Research Project Evaluation: Individual Students, Page 81

You may use this form to evaluate a student's performance on the independent research project. You are asked to assess the student on five basic areas giving a score of 1 to 4. There is also room provided for examples or comments.

Research Project Evaluation: Class Record, Page 82

This form allows you to record the scores on all five basic areas assessed for each student in the class. That way you will know how all students did on the project at a glance. There is also room for you to make a brief comment for each student.

Oral Presentation Evaluation, Page 83

This evaluation form can be used when assessing the oral presentation students make to report their research findings to the class. Students are scored on a variety of public speaking skills. As was mentioned earlier, you may wish to give a copy of this evaluation form to students so they will know in advance how their presentation will be scored.

Current Event Presentation Evaluation, Page 84

This form can be used to evaluate the oral presentation students give when reporting on their current event. Students are assessed on their ability to communicate the facts and significance of the event, if the presentation was interesting and informative, if the student was able to answer questions, and if the student made a personal connection.

Independent Research Contract

Name _____

Date _____

The Project:

My research topic is _____

What do I need to know? _____

Where will I get this information? _____

Time line: (Provide dates.)

I will begin my research _____

I will present a progress report _____

I will conclude my study _____

I will present my final report _____

Presentation:

_____ I will present my research in a paper.

_____ I will do an oral presentation of my research to the class.

_____ I will make a physical project to present my research. (diorama, etc.)

Research Project Cover Sheet

Name _____

Date _____

Topic _____

Title of Research Project:

_____

Describe how effective you were in gathering information for your project. _____

_____

_____

Describe how effective you were in communicating your conclusions.

_____

_____

_____

_____

What do you plan to focus on in your oral presentation? _____

_____

_____

_____

_____

Research Project Evaluation:
Individual Students

Name _____

Research Project _____

(1 = poor 2 = average 3 = good 4 = excellent)

Skill	Score 1	2	3	4
Information obtained from several sources Examples:				
Project meets requirements Examples:				
Extras included (cover, pictures) Examples:				
Oral report given to class Comments:				
Extra credit work Examples:				

Research Project Evaluation: Class Record

Project: _____

Name	Sources	Requirements	Extras	Oral Presentation	Extra Credit	Comments

Oral Presentation Evaluation

```
Name _____ Date _____

Topic _____
```

(Score: 1= poor 2= average 3= good 4= excellent)

1. The student speaks confidently.   Score _____

    Comments: _____

2. The student expresses ideas with fluency.   Score _____

    Comments: _____

3. The student answered questions.   Score _____

    Comments: _____

4. The student used facial expressions while speaking.   Score _____

    Comments: _____

5. The student used a variety of inflections.   Score _____

    Comments: _____

6. The student showed pacing.   Score _____

    Comments: _____

7. The student maintained eye contact with the audience.   Score _____

    Comments: _____

8. The student used appropriate body language and posture.   Score _____

    Comments: _____

    Additional Comments: _____

Current Event Presentation Evaluation

Name _____ Date _____

Topic _____

Did the student convey the basic facts of the event accurately? _____

_____

_____

_____

Did the student convey the significance of the event? _____

_____

_____

_____

_____

Was the presentation both interesting and informative? _____

_____

_____

_____

_____

Was the student able to answer questions about the event? _____

_____

_____

_____

Did the student make a personal connection or convey a personal reaction to the event?

_____

_____ _____

_____

Getting Started

Rationale

Teachers in classrooms across the country are beginning to see learning as a joint venture between the teacher and the student. Naturally, then, the responsibility for evaluation should also be shared between teacher and student. Self-evaluation makes the students aware of their own learning, progress, and growth throughout the school year. It is an indispensable part of any learning and assessment program that strives to have students take responsibility for their own learning.

Self-evaluation requires reflection about not only academic work but also attitude. Perhaps difficulty with social studies concepts has nothing to do with content, but rather everything to do with motivation. By taking time to reflect, students can determine where their strengths and weaknesses lie and how to pinpoint what exactly is causing any difficulty.

How to Use Student Self-Evaluation

We cannot expect students to jump right into self-evaluation, they must be trained. Traditionally, students do the work and wait for the teacher to return it with a letter grade on top. Evaluating your own work is not easy and taking the responsibility for doing so is certainly a challenge. The forms in this resource guide will help students to gradually become engaged in the self-evaluation process. They are asked to reflect on their academic achievement and their attitude, both important learning components.

It is important for you to stress confidentiality with student self-evaluations. Students may be reluctant to self-report and self-assess accurately if they fear their answers will be made public.

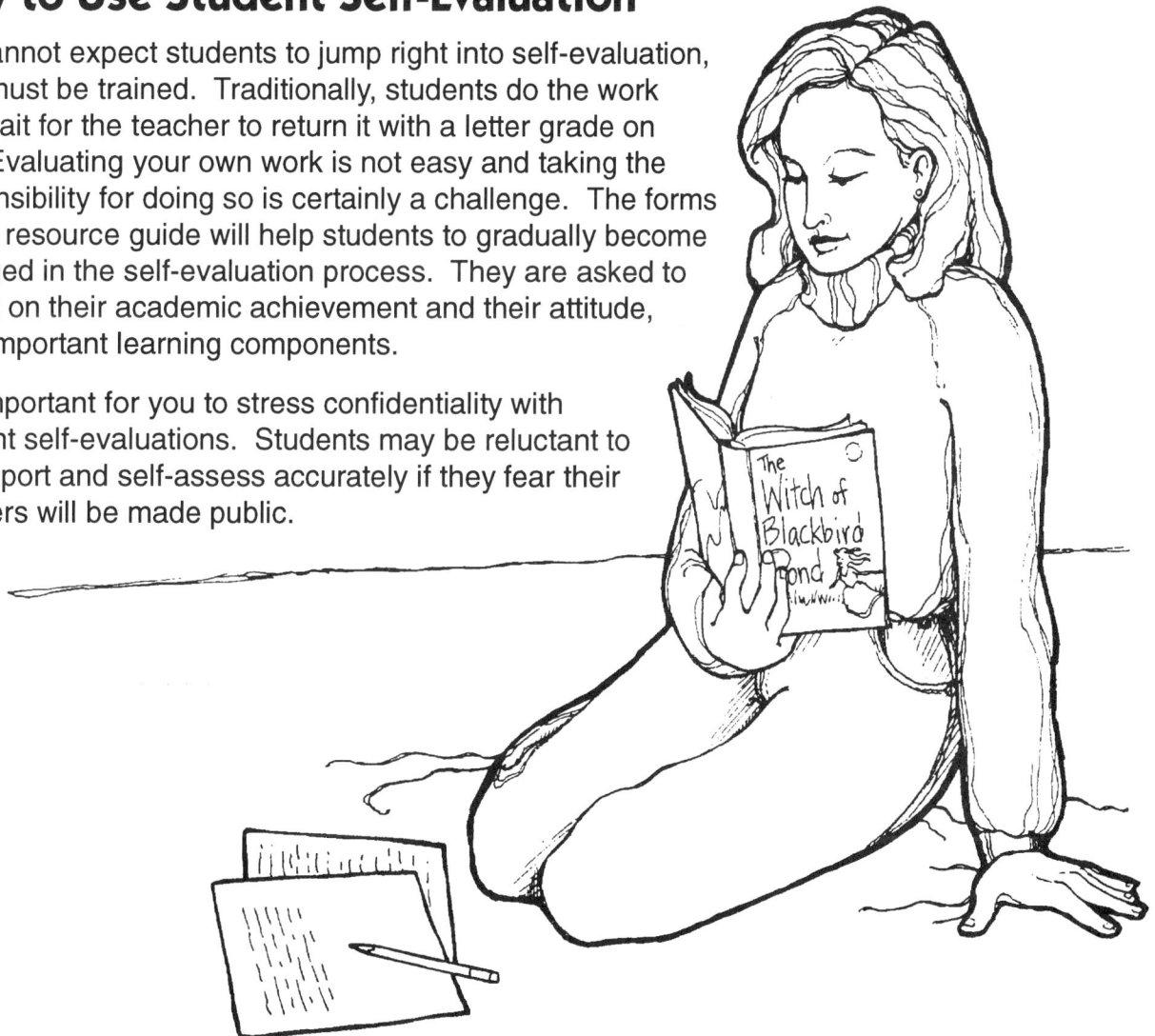

Getting Started *(cont.)* _____

Using the Forms in This Section

Social Studies Concepts Self-Evaluation, Page 87

This form is very useful because it is so flexible. It can be used along with any topic you may be studying in social studies. Students are asked to identify what they already know about the topic they will be studying prior to reading the textbook. Then they are asked to report on what they learned following their reading of the text. Then, they must evaluate what else they need to know about the topic prior to taking a test. This last question can be particularly helpful for test preparation.

Research Project Self-Evaluation, Page 88

This form works very nicely with the other assessment forms in the "Research Project" section of this resource guide. However, because this form is a self-evaluation it has been included in this section. Students are asked to rate their performance in five different areas related to their long term research project. It may be interesting for you to compare the student's response to your own response on the similar form for teachers located in the "Research Project" section on page 81.

Assignment Self-Evaluation, Page 89

This form asks students to evaluate a specific assignment. Students are asked how they feel about the assignment, what they did best, and where they need to improve. They are also asked to give themselves a grade for the assignment and record a goal for their next assignment. Notes students make regarding what needs improvement can be used for future self-evaluations and reflections.

Writing Evaluation for a Publication Piece, Page 90

Now that students are reading so much historical fiction they should be encouraged to write a historical fiction piece of their own. These stories can then be published for the rest of the class to enjoy. When determining which story to publish students can use this writing self-evaluation. This form requires students to justify their selection of a piece of writing for publication. Students are asked why the piece was chosen, what makes it good, what is the strongest part, and what makes it ready for publication.

Social Studies Concepts Self-Evaluation

Name _____ Date_____

Topic of study _____

What do you already know about the topic? (Complete this section prior to reading the textbook)

What did you learn about the topic? (Complete this section after reading the text)

What else do you need to know about the topic? (Complete prior to taking an exam on the topic)

Research Project Self-Evaluation

Name _____ Date_____

Topic of study _____

(1 = poor 2 = average 3 = good 4 = excellent)

	Score			
Skill	**1**	**2**	**3**	**4**
Chose topic Comments:				
Consulted reference books Examples:				
Wrote report to meet requirements Examples:				
Included extras (cover, pictures) Examples:				
Gave oral report Comments:				

88

Assignment Self-Evaluation

Name _____ Date _____

Type of Assignment _____

Title of Assignment _____

1. How do you feel about this assignment? _____

   _____

   _____

2. What did you do best on this assignment? _____

   _____

   _____

3. What could you improve on this assignment? _____

   _____

   _____

4. What was most difficult about this assignment? _____

   _____

   _____

5. What grade do you feel you deserve on this assignment and why?

   _____

   _____

   Goal: On my next assignment...

   _____

   _____

Writing Evaluation for a Publication Piece

Name _____ Date _____

Title of story _____

Historical time period _____

Historical event _____

Why did you choose this story for publication? _____

_____

What makes the story exciting, forceful, or convincing? _____

_____

What is the strongest part of the story? _____

_____

What makes that part so strong? _____

Did you write for a specific audience? _____

What was important to you when you were writing this piece?

_____

_____

What did you wrestle with while writing? _____

_____

_____

Why is your story ready for publication? _____

_____

_____

90

Getting Started

Rationale

We take great pains to keep the parents of our students informed regarding progress and classroom activities. Parents can be invited to take part in the evaluation of the child's growth and progress. By involving parents the assessment cycle is complete because all three participants in the student's education— teacher, student, and parent, have all been involved in evaluation. By asking parents to take a more active role in evaluation, they will naturally become more involved in the student's homework. Home reading logs can help parents to realize when their child is spending too much time playing or watching T.V. rather than reading their social studies text or a piece of historical fiction. Another benefit of parent evaluation is clearly seen at parent conference time. Parents are better informed and better able to discuss their child's progress with you. Now the conference is a two way conversation between teacher and parent, rather than a one way monologue performed by the teacher directed at the parent.

How to Use Parent Evaluations

Parents, like students, need to be adequately trained in how to evaluate. It may be well worth your time to schedule a parent training session after school so parents can be well informed about the process. Although initially it will take time to plan such a training session, in the long run you will get more and better information on the parent response forms.

Using the Forms in This Section

Parent Questionnaire, Page 92

It is important for parents to consider their child's strengths and weaknesses in the classroom. They should also consider what goals they have for their child. This form will help parents get a grasp on the present and future of their child's education.

Home Reading Log, Page 93

Students can use this form to keep track of the textbook chapters and books they read at home as well as the time they spend reading. Parents are asked to verify the entries made by students.

Parent Questionnaire

Student's Name _____

Age_____   Grade_____   Date _____

Name of parent completing form _____

Please answer the questions as they relate to the study of social studies.

1. What is going well for your child this year? _____

   _____

   _____

2. What progress has your child made since the beginning of the school year?

   _____

   _____

3. Do you have any concerns about your child? _____

   _____

   _____

4. Do you have any suggestions for working with your child? _____

   _____

   _____

5. What are your goals for your child this school year? _____

   _____

Additional Comments: _____

_____

Thank you for your time!

92

Parent Evaluation

Home Reading Log

Student's Name _____

Parent Name _____

Please verify the time your child spends reading the social studies text or books related to social studies at home.

Date	Title of Book/Chapter	Pages	Time Start	Time Stop	Parent Sign

Thanks for your time!

CONGRATULATIONS

to

_____

For Outstanding

Achievement

In

_____

_____   _____
Teacher's Signature   Date

Generic Record Sheet

Social Studies Assessment Bibliography

Braun, Joseph A. "Social Technology in the Elementary Social Studies Curriculum." *Social Education*, 1992.

Evans, Michael D. "Manifest Destiny: Understanding Through Simulation." *Social Education,* 1993.

Finkelstein, Judith M., Lynn E. Nielsen, and Thomas Switzer. "Primary Elementary Social Studies Instruction: A Status Report." *Social Education*, 1993.

Goodman, Kenneth S., Lois Bridges Bird, and Yetta M.Goodman. *The Whole Language Catalog Supplement on Authentic Assessment.* Macmillan, 1992.

Gustafson, Kraig. "Government in Action: A Simulation." *Social Education*, 1993.

Herman, Joan L., Pamela R. Aschbacher, and Lynn Winters. "A Practical Guide to Alternative Assessment." *Association for Supervision and Curriculum Development*, 1992.

Hill, Bonnie Campbell. *Practical Aspects of Authentic Assessment: Putting the Pieces Together.* Christopher-Gordon Publishers, 1994.

Jasmine, Julia. *Portfolio Assessment for Your Whole Language Classroom.* Teacher Created Materials, 1992.

Jasmine, Julia. *Portfolios and Other Assessments.* Teacher Created Materials, 1993.

Marzano, Robert J., Debra Pickering, and Jay McTighe. *Assessing Student Outcomes.* Association for Supervision and Curriculum Development, 1993.

Perrone, Vito. *Expanding Student Assessment.* Association for Supervision and Curriculum Development, 1993.

Routman, Regie. *Invitations.* Heinemann, 1991.

Routman, Regie. *Transitions.* Heinemann, 1988.

Tierney, Robert J., Mark A. Carter, and Laura E. Desai. *Portfolio Assessment in the Reading-Writing Classroom.* Christopher Gordon Publishers, 1991.

Tunnell, Michael O., and Richard Ammon, (Eds.). *The Story of Ourselves: Teaching History Through Children's Literature.* Heinemann, 1993.